The Magic School Bus
Inside a Hurricane

The Magic School Bus
Inside a Hurricane

By Joanna Cole
Illustrated by Bruce Degen

SCHOLASTIC INC.
New York   Toronto   London   Auckland   Sydney

The author and illustrator wish to thank Dr. Robert C. Sheets,
Director of the National Hurricane Center; and Dr. Daniel Leathers, Delaware State Climatologist,
University of Delaware for their assistance in preparing this book.

ISBN 0-590-44687-8

12 11 10 9 8 7 6 5 4 3 2 1   6 7 8 9/9 0 1/0

Printed in the U.S.A.   08

The illustrator used pen and ink, watercolor, color pencil,
and gouache for the paintings in this book.

Production supervision by Angela Biola
Designed by Bruce Degen

She's the Magic School Bus Editor
And we'd like herewith to credit her:
To Phoebe Yeh
Our Sunny Day.

J.C. & B.D.

Have you heard about our teacher, Ms. Frizzle?
Her clothes are wild, her school bus is wacky,
and her class trips are weird.
Whenever we study something in her class,
we get into it in a *really* big way.

We were learning about weather.
Absolutely everything in our room
was about rain or snow or sun or wind.
Every kid in the class
was doing a weather project.
We were even listening to
weather reports on Ms. Frizzle's radio.

We hadn't finished our experiments about air, but with Frizzie at the wheel, we were going — ready or not!

SORRY, I CAN'T GO, MS. FRIZZLE. I HAVE TO SHARPEN MY PENCIL.

BUT ARNOLD, MAYBE WE'LL HAVE A REAL ADVENTURE.

IN THAT CASE, I HAVE TO SHARPEN SEVERAL PENCILS.

LOOK FOR A CHANGE IN THE WEATHER, FOLKS.

Q: WHEN DOES THE WEATHER CHANGE?
A: WHEN THE AIR CHANGES
by Shirley
1. Is the air hot or cold?
2. Is it dry or moist?
3. Is it still or moving?
When these things change, the weather changes!

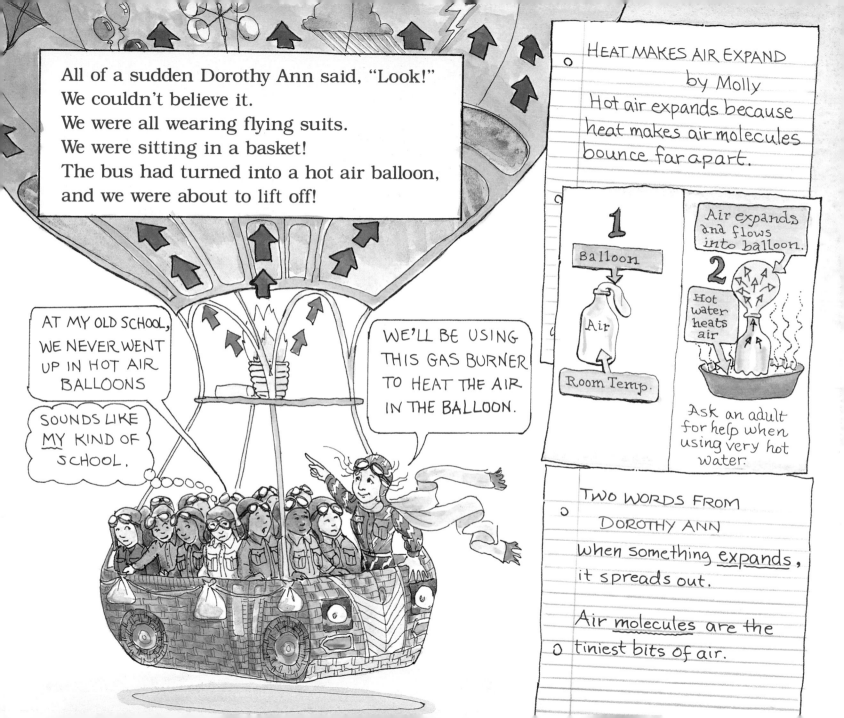

We started going up, and Ms. Frizzle said, "Did I mention, children, that hot air rises?"

We rose higher and higher.
Even though hot air was filling the balloon,
the air around us was growing colder.
We had to put on warm jackets.

GOING UP?
BETTER BUNDLE UP!
by Phoebe

BRRR.

Warm air rises
from earth.
As it goes up,
it gets colder.

IT'S COLD UP HERE!

YOU'RE NOT AFRAID
OF HIGH PLACES,
ARE YOU, ARNOLD?

THAT RADIO SPOKE TO ME!

HOW DID IT KNOW MY
NAME?

I KNEW I SHOULD HAVE
STAYED HOME TODAY.

YOU CAN'T SEE IT,
BUT IT'S ALL
AROUND YOU.
WHAT IS IT?

Riddle
Book

AIR!

A WEATHER WORD
by Dorothy Ann
When water condenses, molecules of water vapor join together and make drops of liquid water.

"Warm air rising from earth carries lots of water vapor molecules," Ms. Frizzle continued.
"As the air rises, it cools down. The water condenses in the air and forms clouds."

DID YOU BRING YOUR RAINCOAT, ARNOLD?

TELL ME THIS ISN'T HAPPENING....

We drifted into the center of a cloud.
Ms. Frizzle was right — it was *damp* in there.
The cloud was made of tiny water droplets
hanging in the air.

Down below, the weather forecasters were standing in the rain.
They didn't see us inside the cloud, but we could hear their voices.
One of them said, "I hope that teacher knows there's a *hurricane watch* in effect."

WHAT IS A HURRICANE?
by Florrie
A hurricane is one of the most violent kinds of storms.
In a hurricane, winds swirl in a circle around the storm's center at 74 miles per hour or more!

HURRICANE SYMBOL

MORE WORDS FROM DOROTHY ANN
A Hurricane Watch means that a hurricane may strike within the next 36 hours.
A Hurricane Warning means that a hurricane is likely to strike within the next 24 hours.
A warning is more urgent than a watch.

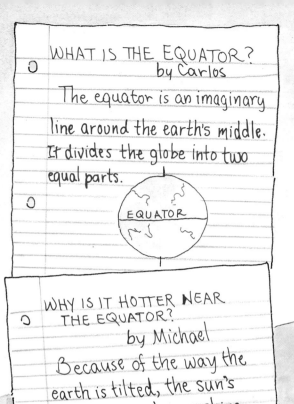

WHAT IS THE EQUATOR?
by Carlos

The equator is an imaginary line around the earth's middle. It divides the globe into two equal parts.

EQUATOR

WHY IS IT HOTTER NEAR THE EQUATOR?
by Michael

Because of the way the earth is tilted, the sun's rays almost always shine toward the earth's middle. This means there are no cold winters there.

SUN · MOST DIRECT RAYS · NORTH POLE · EQUATOR · SOUTH POLE · THE TROPICS

As usual, Ms. Frizzle paid no attention.
She turned up the fire, and more
hot air rushed into the balloon.
As we rose above the cloud,
the wind started pushing us south.
Before long, we had traveled thousands of miles.
Ms. Frizzle said we were above a tropical ocean
about five hundred miles north of the equator.

WOW! LOOK AT THAT WATER!

WE CAN GO SWIMMING!

AND WINDSURFING!

AND SNORKELING!

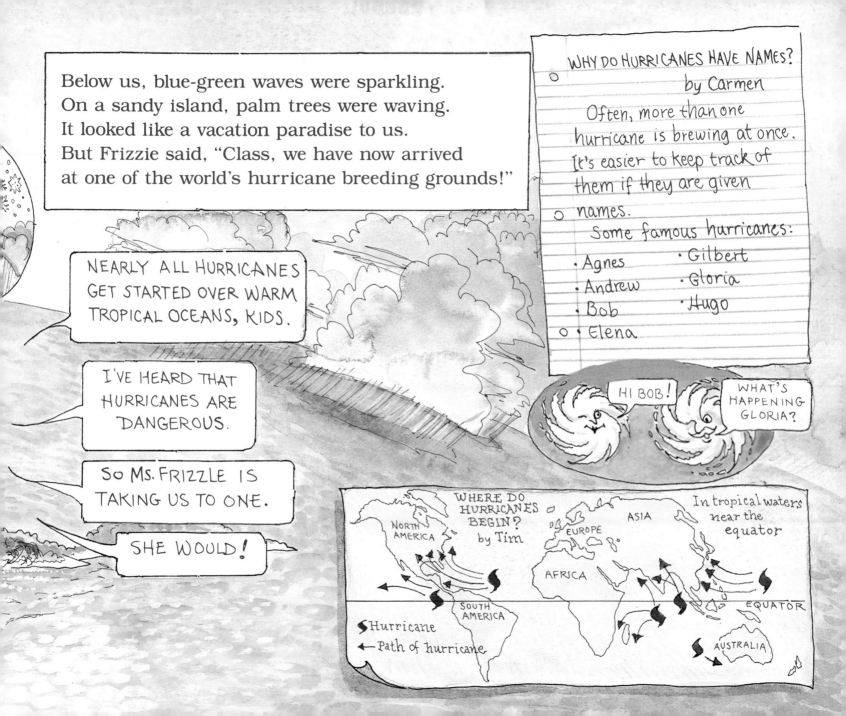

WHEN IS HURRICANE SEASON?
by Rachel

Most hurricanes begin in the late summer and early fall. That is when tropical oceans are warmest.

The warmer the ocean is, the stronger the hurricane is likely to become.

"Class, remember that as hot air rises from the ocean surface, the water vapor in the air condenses and forms clouds," said the Friz.
Down below, more hot air rushed in from all sides to take the place of the rising air.
In the middle of the rising air, a column of sinking air formed.
We started sinking with it.

AUGUST   SEPTEMBER   OCTOBER

WATER VAPOR CONDENSES

AIR COOLS THEN SINKS

WARM, MOIST AIR RISES

A HURRICANE IS STARTING!

OUR BALLOON IS FALLING!

OH, NO!

SINKING AIR

WINDS   WINDS

RAIN   RAIN

WARM, MOIST AIR BLOWS

WARM OCEAN SURFACE

WHAT MAKES HURRICANE
WINDS BLOW IN A CIRCLE?
by Alex

Winds begin by blowing straight. But the movement of the earth as it spins on its axis makes them curve.

WINDS CURVE

THE EARTH SPINS →

AXIS

The faster winds blow, the more they curve. Hurricane winds are very fast, so they curve and curve until they make a circle.

The wind was blowing the clouds into a huge circle.
"The storm is starting to take on the typical shape of a hurricane. Isn't it fascinating, children?" shouted Ms. Frizzle.

HELP!

WE'RE GOING AROUND IN CIRCLES!

I'M GETTING DIZZY!

It was more than fascinating.
It was terrifying!
We were caught in the edge of the storm,
blowing around and around in a giant whirlwind.
That whirlwind was a hurricane!

A TYPICAL HURRICANE HAS A LIFE SPAN OF ABOUT 10 DAYS.

LISTENERS— WE'LL BE TELLING YOU ABOUT THE WHOLE HURRICANE.

MAYBE ITS BATTERIES WILL RUN OUT SOON.

HOW BIG IS A HURRICANE?
by John
Hurricanes are enormous. Each one is about 10 miles high and 300 to 600 miles wide!

Where We Are in the Hurricane

In the clouds around us,
huge bolts of lightning were flashing.
We thought it was all over for us,
but then we saw the bus again.
It had become a weather plane —
the kind that explores hurricanes.
We tumbled into a rescue chute
and fell onto the plane . . . that is,
the bus . . . er . . . we mean the plane.

Ms. Frizzle marked Arnold absent and flew straight into the storm.

All around were columns of air
called hot towers, or chimneys.
They were sucking up more and more
hot moist air from the ocean.
The heat energy from the air
was feeding the storm
and making it stronger.
The plane was shaking
and so were we!

IT'S QUIET IN THE EYE OF A
HURRICANE
                    by Carlos
    The fierce swirling winds
of the hurricane do not
enter the center of the
storm.

WINDS   WINDS

Land
Arnold
Eye   Eye wall
Where we are in the Hurricane

Then suddenly everything was quiet.
"Class, we have entered the eye — or center —
of the hurricane!" announced Ms. Frizzle.
The ocean waves still crashed below
and the winds howled outside,
but in the eye only gentle breezes blew.
Up above, the sky was blue
and the sun was shining.
We relaxed and enjoyed ourselves.

PEACE AND QUIET!

BALMY BREEZES!

A·A·AH!

We flew about thirty miles
across the eye.
Then the Friz called out,
"We will enter the other side
of the eye wall now."
"Don't go!" we cried,
but the plane was already
on its way — back into the
hurricane's fierce wind and rain.

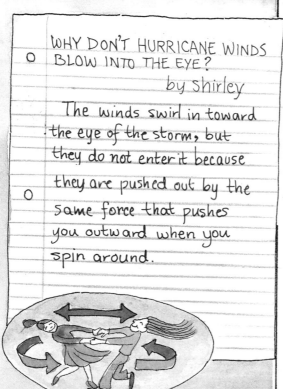

WHY DON'T HURRICANE WINDS
BLOW INTO THE EYE?
by shirley

The winds swirl in toward
the eye of the storm, but
they do not enter it because
they are pushed out by the
same force that pushes
you outward when you
spin around.

WE'RE TRYING TO REACH LAND BEFORE THE FULL FORCE OF THE HURRICANE HITS!

GOOD IDEA!

THE HURRICANE IS APPROACHING LAND. THERE WILL BE HEAVY FLOODING ALONG THE COAST.

HOW HURRICANES TRAVEL
by Wanda

When a hurricane starts, it usually moves slowly—about 10 to 20 miles per hour. As the storm gets farther north, its speed can increase up to 60 miles per hour! Hurricanes can travel hundreds of miles each day.

WHICH PART OF THE HURRICANE IS STRONGEST?
by Florrie

The right front corner is strongest because the whirling winds are circling toward the shore. They add their strength to the winds that move the storm forward.

The entire hurricane was moving across the ocean toward land, and we were going with it!
"The right forward corner of the hurricane as you are looking toward land has the strongest wind and rain and the highest ocean waves," shouted the Friz. Naturally, she flew directly into that part.

A HURRICANE MOVES LIKE A TOP SPINNING ACROSS THE FLOOR.

IT MOVES TWO WAYS—

IT SPINS AROUND...

...AND, IT TRAVELS FORWARD.

SPEED 25 LIMIT

Most damage will be done here

LAND

EYE

STORM'S LEFT FRONT

STORM'S RIGHT FRONT

RIGHT REAR

LEFT REAR

FORWARD STORM MOVEMENT

ANOTHER WEATHER WORD
by Dorothy Ann
When people evacuate an area, they get out of there fast!

But that was nothing compared to the horror we felt when we heard the Friz shouting above the sound of roaring water,
"We seem to be running out of gas, children!"
Sure enough, the plane was dipping lower and lower.

As we fell into the water, we saw Arnold waving to us from a nearby roof.

Somehow Arnold managed to get on the plane
before we were swept away by the waves
at the front edge of the hurricane.
The water was creeping up the windows.
The plane was going to sink for sure!
Then we saw a dark, funnel shape coming our way.

After a while we felt a bump and looked around.
The tornado had set us down gently.
We were in our old school bus again.
We were dressed in our regular clothes again.
The hurricane was over.
And we were at a gas station.

Ms. Frizzle filled up the tank
and drove down the road
as if nothing had happened.
"As I said earlier, class, we are on our way
to visit a weather station," she said.

TAKE OUR CASE,
FOR EXAMPLE.
WE'RE ALL OKAY.

EVEN THE RADIO IS
STILL WORKING FINE.

HERE'S A TREAT JUST
FOR YOU, ARNOLD—
ANOTHER WEATHER
UPDATE....

THAT DEPENDS ON
WHAT YOU MEAN
BY "WORKING FINE."

GAS

The weather forecasters at the station had a lot to tell us about hurricanes. *We* had a lot to tell *them*, too!

Finally, we drove back to school
and finished up our weather projects.

After that trip, we needed some time to relax.
Ms. Frizzle said we could have a party.
We had great games, crazy dancing, and yummy snacks.
And for a while, we didn't even think about
Ms. Frizzle's next class trip!

The Magic School Bus Mail Bag
Letters... we get letters...

To the Magic School Bus Editor:
You should not have said that a school bus could turn into a hot air balloon or a weather plane. That cannot really happen.   Your friend, Sam

EXOTIC BROOKLYN

FOR SALE

Dear Joanna,
Radios cannot have conversations with people.

Barbara

TO: JOANNA COLE
AUTHOR
c/o Scholastic Inc.

GREETINGS FROM SUNNY EAST ORANGE, N.J.

Dear Joanna and Bruce,
Reading about hurricanes may be fun, but it is no fun to be in one!
I know because my family was in Hurricane ANDREW and it was scary!

~ Keith

Dear Bruce,
Radios do not dance.

from Jean

TO: Bruce Degen
ARTIST
c/o Scholastic Inc.

Dear Arnold,
On your trip, the hurricane reached land. But most hurricanes go far out to sea and do not hurt people and property.
Your friend,
Al, the weather scientist

A fishing boat probably would not survive if it were out in a very strong hurricane.
From the Coast Guard

To all readers:
Some of the things that happen in this book are make-believe. But of course, all the Science is real!

Joanna & Bruce

Dear Ms. Frizzle,
We think the whole class should enroll in Phoebe's old school.
—The students at the Better-Safe-than-Sorry School

MOONLIGHT IN BURBANK

Winter in Connecticut

Dear Joanna,
The things that happen on Ms. Frizzle's trips are much too risky for children. Please keep them home next time.

Your Mother

Dear Bruce,
If Arnold really fell from a great height into the ocean, he would need medical attention!

From your Doctor

MSB CENTRAL

MAIL

MSB